SALES LEADERSHIP MASTERY

Learn to Set Smart Goals, Develop a Growth Mindset, Manage Your Time Effectively, and Build a Successful Life

by

J P PATHAK

Email: jppathak1@gmail.com

Copyright © 2024 by J P Pathak

All rights reserved. No part of this book may be reproduced in any form without permission in writing from the author.

No part of this publication may be reproduced or transmitted in any form or by any means, mechanical or electronic, including photocopying or recording, by any information storage and retrieval system, or by email or any other means whatsoever without permission in writing from the author.

DEDICATION

To all my Pharma colleagues and friends,

Your unwavering support, solidarity, and shared vision have been the cornerstone of my journey. Each one of you has contributed to my growth and has been an inspiration in countless ways.

And to my esteemed mentor,

Your guidance, wisdom, and belief in my potential have shaped me into the leader I am today. Your mentorship has been invaluable, and for that, I am eternally grateful.

This book is a testament to the collective strength, knowledge, and experience we have shared. May it serve as a beacon of inspiration for all who seek to lead with integrity and passion.

With Love and Gratitude.

J P Pathak

ACKNOWLEDGMENT

I am deeply grateful to my former colleagues, and friends, whose unwavering support and solidarity have been the foundation for my journey. You have contributed to my growth and inspired me in countless ways.

A special thank you to my esteemed mentor, whose guidance, wisdom, and belief in my potential have shaped me into the leader I am today. Your mentorship has been invaluable, and for that , I am eternally grateful.

To my family, for their endless love and patience, and to all who believed in me, your encouragement and understanding have made this book possible.

Thank you all for being part of this journey.

With warm regards,

J P Pathak

WHY IS THIS BOOK FOR YOU?

Welcome back to the 'Rise and Thrive' series, where we embark on a journey of personal and professional growth guided by the wisdom of Ramdas, our steadfast guide and companion in this seventh episode, we delve deeper into the principles of success and fulfillment, exploring the transformative power of goal setting in sales leadership.

As we reunite with Ramdas, we find ourselves in the bustling city of Mumbai, where our protagonist Varun grapples with doubts and uncertainties amidst the demands of his sales career. Through Varun's story, we witness the universal struggle of navigating ambition and self-doubt in pursuit of greatness.

Join us as we follow Varun's journey of self-discovery and growth, guided by the timeless wisdom of Ramdas, Together, we will uncover the secrets of setting SMART goals, fostering a growth mindset, and building high-performing teams. Through triumphs and setbacks, challenges and victories, we'll learn valuable lessons in resilience, leadership, and the pursuit of excellence.

Let us embark on this journey of discovery and transformation, as we rise above our limitations and thrive in the pursuit of our goals. Ramdas awaits us, ready to light the path ahead with his wisdom and guidance. Are you ready to join us on this adventure?

With Regards,

J P Pathak

Table Of Contents

Purpose of Life and Clarity of Vision 13
- Role of Training 15
- Exercise 19
- Skill Development 19
- Summary 23
- Proven Sales Processes 24
- Exercise 27

Goal Setting 29
- Storytime 30
- Exercise 34
- How to Set Goals? 34
- Key takeaways 37

Developing a Growth Mindset 39
- Storytime 40
- Why is Growth Midset Crucial for Success? 42
- Embracing Challenges 42
- Cultivating and Nurturing high-performing teams 45
- Summary 46

Effective Sales Strategies 47
- Storytime 49
- A. Consultative Selling 52
- B. Spin Selling 57
- C. Value Selling 60
- D. Social Selling 62

    E. Relationship Selling 63

    Summary 66

    Key takeaway 66

Building a High-Performing Sales Team 69

    Importance of A High-Performing Team 69

    Storytime 70

    Exercise 75

Leveraging Technology and Data in Sales 79

Continuous Learning and Development in Sales Technology 83

Future Trends in Sales Technology 85

Nurturing Customer Relationships 89

    Storytime 89

Leveraging Technology and Data for Enhanced Customer Insights 93

    Pharma Marketing 94

Nurturing Customer Relationships 97

    Storytime 97

Achieving Work-life Balance 101

Effective Time Management 107

    Key Techniques for Effective Time Management 107

    Key takeaways 111

Continuous Learning and Professional Development ... 115

    Key Points 115

Summary 121

About The Author 123

Other Books Written By The Author 125
Disclaimer 127
May I Ask You A Favor? 129

Purpose of Life and Clarity of Vision

Varun was from a small village and had seen poverty very closely he had friends who had the prospect of a full meal as a luxury. A few occasions like marriage parties or small village functions were these luxurious days for them.

Varun was dreaming of helping his friends and helping them to lead a better life. He was fascinated by stories of successful leaders. He knew the importance of education but for them, it was a distant concept. The village lacked even a basic school, leaving the children with little hope for a different future.

One fine day Varun went to his maternal uncle and saw a school building for the first time. He was so excited to see the school with boys and girls having books in their hands. Their faces lit with joy of learning. He was mesmerized and inspired by the sight. The school's headmaster, noticing the spark in the eyes of Varun, spoke to his uncle and asked him to bring Varun to school the next day. The headmaster spoke to Varun and discovered his eagerness to learn. Recognizing Varun's potential, the headmaster decided to sponsor his education and asked his uncle to ensure that Varun came to school the next day,

With a new world of possibilities opening up before him, Varun embraced this opportunity with zeal. He studied diligently, driven by the desire to find his purpose and uplift his friends back In his village. His journey was not that easy.

He came to the city after getting basic schooling in his uncle's village. He got a scholarship so fees and books were not an issue for him but other basic needs made Varun's life far from easy. During his college days, Varun had many sleepless nights, he often slept on a railway platform. The financial struggles were severe, but Varun's commitment never wavered.

You might have heard, that God helps those who help themselves. This was so true with Varun. One day he was caught by a ticket collector at the Railway station and he brought Varun to his Head TC. Who listened to Varun's story and was so impressed by his vision and decided to support Varun,. He gave him a room in his house, with the condition that he would give home tuition to his children. Varun won the hearts of everyone there and was like a family member to them. With the help of his uncle, Ramdas, and Head TC, Varun graduated with honors and secured a job as a sales executive in a pharmaceutical company. That is how I met Varun and learned about his life.

Despite his hardships, Varun never lost sight of his vision: to help his village. He diligently saved a portion of his earnings and returned to his roots. Using the money he saved, Varun established the village's first school. His once-dreaming friends now had the chance for their kids to learn, dream, and aspire for a better future.

Varun's journey from a small village boy to a successful professional underscores the transformative power of education and the importance of having a clear vision and purpose in life. If you have determination, support, and a clear sense of purpose in life, then you can overcome even the most daunting obstacles and make a significant impact on society.

Remember:

Education can be a powerful tool to change lives and uplift communities,

If you have a clear purpose in life then you can achieve great things,

Stay focused on your long-term goals.

While working closely with Varun, I understood that it was not just a personal success of Varun but about giving back to the community and creating opportunities for others.

Clarity of vision and a sense of purpose are essential for true success and fulfillment.

Role of Training

During one of the meetings, I asked Varun to share his learnings and what made him a successful salesperson. His response was very simple.

1- Have clear goals

2- Have plans to achieve your goals

3- Have a hunger for success

4- Be empathetic

5- Be competitive

6- Have networking abilities

7- Be confident

8- Be enthusiastic and

9- Be resilient

10- Be a life-long learner

I was impressed by his understanding and over time I noticed that Varun was much ahead of his competitors he was the competition to others and he had no competition at all.

I learned that Varun was a highly skilled salesperson and trusted customer advisor. He saves for his community, his future, and at the same time his personal development.

Varun was able to make out very fast about the needs of his customers. He was using customer psychology to engage his customers. 'Psychology helps to understand better how customers think, feel, and behave'.

I used this opportunity to learn more about Varun's success. My next question to him was –Varun can you please tell me more about customer psychology and how did you learn that?

Varun's response brought clarity and I developed a respect for his interest and his clarity of vision. He said I read many books and articles on customer psychology. I developed my own understanding while knowing about customer behaviors. For example-

How customers choose a brand

What motivates them to choose brand 'x' or brand 'y'

Role of personal relationship in choosing a brand. And I pay a lot of attention to reading the emotions of my customers.

I asked Varun, Is there any role of training in your success? He became a little serious and continued, It was training and my training manager who made a big difference, and I could read his emotions when he said 'My Training Manager' and not training manager. I missed the opportunity in the beginning as my manager was more concerned about sales and not the development of his team so did not nominate me for the training but my training under a new leader made a world of difference for me. I was better in product knowledge and learned selling skills which are critical for success. I am a product of training and my clarity of purpose.

I insisted on sharing more about product knowledge and sales techniques. Varun was very enthusiastic about sharing his learning and his professional growth. I always suggest my participants to be a good and active listener. It always helps to develop not only good understanding but good relationships too.

It was after field work and really a hectic day but a cup of hot coffee and my appreciation to Varun's success brought joy to his face and he shared the following-

A- Product Knowledge: I understood during a training program, Varun said, that an in-depth understanding of my product is crucial. Training helped me to effectively communicate the features, benefits, and unique selling points of my brand. Earlier I was not clear about the difference between features and benefits and was making mistakes during my presentation to my customers. Sounds very interesting Varun, why don't you share about features and benefits with us? His new young energetic and enthusiastic leader also joined us over a cup of coffee.

He took a minute and shared:

Feature: The technical or factual part of a product. It describes what it does or has. For example, your smartphone has 108 meg pixel camera with night mode capabilities

Advantage: An advantage is what that feature does, and how it helps. These are factual and descriptive but do not yet make a connection as to how it will make users' life better. For example Sharp and clear photos

Benefit: With a 108-megapixel camera you can take professional-quality photos that capture every detail even in low light.

How do I communicate with customers Varun? With a smile on his face, confident Varun looked at his leader and said, Sir, with this Phone equipped with a 108-megapixel camera, you will never miss an important moment, and you can relive your memories in vivid clarity. It can be a family gathering, your sales meeting with the team, or an award function, your photos will always look amazing.

Amazing Varun, we both said with pride in saying so to Varun.

Exercise

Please take a real-time example of your product and write the features, advantages, and benefits of that product.

Brand:

Features:

Advantage:

Benefits:

Skill Development

I learned various sales techniques and improved a lot, for example –How to do prospecting, when to close a call, how to handle objections raised by my customers, and how to complete sales. Mastery of these skills has directly impacted my sales performance and I am better than others because I am doing these things better and am open to learning new techniques every day.

That is wonderful Varun and I would like to suggest a few more things from my side to make you a better salesperson today and an effective leader tomorrow. Varun and his leaders accepted my proposal and I scheduled a structured session with all his team members the next day.

My suggestions to Varun and his colleagues were as follows-

1. Be adaptive and Innovative: I started with Innovation and explained to them that innovation does not necessarily mean creating something entirely new. Instead, it often involves finding new ways to use existing ideas or processes to achieve better results. Time is changing very fast, there are constant changes in market trends, consumer behavior, and technology. So it is important to stay updated and adapt to these changes first and be fast. If you just look back and note – what Pandemic has brought changes in our lives and how we had to change and adapt to new technologies. How digital marketing has changed the perception and is contributing in a big way.

2. Communication Mastery: Effective communication and relationship-building skills are fundamental in sales. These skills will help you to connect better with your customers and understand their needs. Persuasive communication helps you close deals more effectively and build long-term customer relationships.

3. Motivation and Confidence: Knowledge boosts confidence and skills make you more self-assured in your interactions. Motivation is all about identifying your Motive and then taking action to be more successful.

4. Consistency: Consistency is the key to sustained success. Consistency builds trust with customers, ensures steady performance, and creates a reliable foundation for long-term growth. One of the participants asked a very simple but thought-provoking question, "Is consistency about doing the same thing again and again?" I took the opportunity to explain, as I could tell that many of the participants agreed about consistency. "It is about your commitment and staying honest to it, despite obstacles." John Maxwell said," Small disciplines repeated with consistency every day lead to great achievements gained slowly over time."

5. Follow Processes: first you must know the sales processes that work best for you and your team. From prospecting to closing deals, clear processes and repeatable actions help maintain quality and efficiency. We will discuss proven sales processes in detail in the next chapter.

6. Have Realistic Goals: The goal must be SMART- Specific, Measurable, Achievable, Realistic, and Time-bound. As a leader, you should believe in achievable but ambitious goals. Break down larger objectives into smaller, manageable tasks that will keep your team focused and motivated.

Let me give you an example of an Achievable yet Ambitious Goal.

If your industry is growing at 10% annually and you aim to increase sales revenue by 15% in one year, this goal is achievable based on a realistic assessment and market conditions. I always suggest team leaders see the historical growth rates of your company and design a strategy so this target of 15% growth is within reach.

Then what is ambitious?

Suppose your management is asking you for a 20% increase in sales revenue over the previous year's performance, then this is an ambitious goal.

Achieving this goal will require innovative strategies, enhanced sales techniques, and a concerted effort from the entire team.

It is achievable yet ambitious. Take the following steps to make it happen-

- A- Analyse past performance data, identify high-potential markets, and focus on high-margin products. Now help the team devise a realistic strategy to achieve this growth,
- B- Invest in Sales Training to equip sales teams with the skills needed to convert more customers and increase their average order size.
- C- Ask for Marketing Support to run targeted campaigns that can generate more leads, which the sales team can convert into revenue.
- D- Use technology for data analytics, and sales automation to improve the team's efficiency.

Suggested steps:

Break down the annual goal into smaller quarterly targets to make it more manageable and to allow for regular progress tracking. You should not wait for a long to review or evaluate progress, it may be too late in some cases.

Align the Sales Team so everyone understands the goal and their individual roles in achieving it. Provide them with the necessary resources and support.

Hold monthly meetings to review progress, address challenges, and adjust strategies as needed. And

Never miss an opportunity to celebrate success. Even small successes can help maintain team motivation and momentum.

Summary

Setting goals should be done in a way that they are ambitious yet achievable. By challenging your team to push their limits while providing a clear, structured path to success, you can maintain motivation and drive. This approach leads to significant growth and development for both the team and the organization.

I suggested to his leader that on-the-job training schedules and structured classroom personal development programs be implemented for ambitious young professionals like Varun. This way, aspiring leaders in the team can receive the necessary training and development opportunities

.My focus is always on elements of personal development, such as leadership training, time management, effective communication, and goal setting., these are valuable for overall career growth.

Learning from Varun was useful for all the participants when he said, I always spend more time to understand the needs of my customers. This helps him in designing personalized and effective sales strategies.

I always empathize with professionals to build trust and rapport with customers. This always results in higher customer satisfaction and loyalty.

Key Suggestion: Always assess each team member's contribution, provide feedback on their strengths, and identify areas for improvement. Track progress regularly.

Remember: By investing in comprehensive training programs you can ensure your sales team is skilled, adaptable, motivated, and capable of achieving their sales targets and career aspirations.

Proven Sales Processes

I always insist on this, and it has been proven time and time again that leaders who follow the sales process and adopt structured and well-defined sales processes are more successful than others. I have learned from my seniors, mentors, and successful colleagues that they were following these processes;

Identify Target Market: They all were having ideal customer profile for their brands, and accordingly they have done market segmentation. They were using various methods to stay in touch with their potential customers, for example- Cold calling, exchanging pleasantry on social media, and other networking methods to generate leads.

Relationship Building: They all have this trait in common. Their approach may be different but the objective was always the same. The best way to build a relationship is try to understand the needs of your potential customers and also build stronger relationships with existing customers so they are your loyal customers and can refer you to others.

They were all active listeners, capable of gathering valuable insights and demonstrating empathy with their customers through active listening techniques.

They had a common response - Hey, we are never in a hurry and always spend adequate time with our customers to understand their pain points, needs, and objectives.

Based on my understanding and experience I suggest you follow this technique to encourage prospects to share more information so you can easily uncover their pain areas, their real needs, and objectives.

AMTL: Ask More Tell Less. ask open-ended questions and you will be a winner.

Let me give you 2 examples here-

1. Can you tell me about the biggest challenges your team is currently facing in achieving set targets for your key brands?

2. What are your top priorities and goals for this year, and what obstacles are preventing you from achieving them?

Think over question no 1- if I ask you this question then, you can see I am trying to know your struggles. I can provide valuable insights into your pain points and how my product or service might address your pain points.,

With the help of 2nd question, I can always identify the key objectives and the barriers you are encountering. I will try to tailor my solution to meet your specific needs and help you overcome these obstacles.

As you have noted rightly- Active Listening is the key to the success

Every customer is unique and so are their needs, you must address their specific needs and challenges of your customers.

Highlight the unique features, and benefits of your product or service, focusing on how it solves the prospect's/customer's problems.

Exercise

Anticipate a few objections you may face during your presentation to your prospects.

1:

2:

3:

Now. Develop responses to address these concerns effectively.

My suggestion: "Emphasize the value and benefits of the product or service."

Closing the Sales: your prospects will give you some verbal and non-verbal cues that you need to identify. These cues indicate the prospect is ready to make a decision.

This is the time to close the sales and take commitment from your customer/prospect.

Believe in the success mantra- sales never close so have a follow-up plan for these customers. Continue to nurture the relationship through regular communication, support, and value-added services.

Try to get repeat sales, and add a new product or service. Build long-term partnerships.

Remember: "By Following a proven sales process, you can drive consistent performance and achieve sustained success."

Believe in what Eleanor Roosevelt said- "You must do things you think you cannot do"

Start doing and now let us move to effective goal setting.

Goal Setting

"A dream becomes a goal when action is taken toward its achievement."

- Bo Bennett

Goal setting is very important for professionals because your goals keep you focused and motivated. In my career, I have met many people who are not able to distinguish between goals and daily routines. They are doing something for their personal development and they understand them as their goals. Goals should be realistic, achievable, and ambitious.

If you set goals that are too easy, you won't be motivated to put in much effort. On the other hand, if your goals are extremely difficult, you might not even take action. Therefore, your goals should be challenging enough to motivate you to stretch and put in more effort to achieve them.

Example of an Easy Goal-

I will go for a walk for 15 minutes daily.

Are there any challenges to this goal? It does not require much effort or commitment. So this will not motivate you.

Example of a Very Difficult Goal: I will run a marathon in the next 90 days with no prior training.

Is it realistic? This will discourage you from taking any action, may lead to frustration, and will not motivate you as this goal is extremely difficult and unrealistic for someone without any training.

Remember: "Goals that are too easy won't drive you to grow, and too difficult goals can be discouraging." Aim for goals that are both challenging and achievable. These goals will motivate you to push your limits and work hard to succeed.

Let us discuss SMART Goals and the process of goal-setting

"What you get by achieving your goals is not as important as what you become by achieving your goals"

- Zig Ziglar

Storytime

I remember the time when I first learned about goals and goal setting during a discussion between Ramdas and his Guru Ji in my village. It was the beginning of the winter season and people used to gather at a common place to discuss political issues and other general problems the society was facing at that time. On that evening, people were talking about Ramdas' role in helping society overcome the fear of dacoits. His Guru Ji joined the group, and they were planning for a play in the village to celebrate the success. The discussion revolved around which play to organize and who would participate. Some suggested having a play on Ramayana and others on Mahabharata. During that conversation, someone asked a simple question about why some highly skilled and talented people find themselves frustrated, which led to my first lessons on goal setting.I found this question very common among many of the participants I met in my professional journey later.

Guru Ji took center stage, and it was almost like a play with many people participating with great enthusiasm. Guru Ji addressed a question raised by a villager in a unique way. He created a scene from the Epic Mahabharata and invited Ramdas and his friends to participate in order to get the best answer. The scene depicted Arjuna learning archery with his Guru (Saga).Dronacharya.

Saga Dronacharya asked Arjuna, What is your goal, young archer?

"I want to be the best archer in the kingdom," Arjuna replied.

Guru Ji with a well known smile on his face asked Ramdas and friends," What is being the 'best' mean to you? He further said- This goal is admirable but vague. Do you all agree was another question from him to the group?

There was a silence in the air and Guru Ji asked again, is it winning every competition is clear or hitting the bullseye every time that can be said as the 'best'? In the chorus, the response was- hitting the bullseye every time is the meaning of 'best'.

My learning that day was- "You should have **clear** and **specific** goals"

Guru Ji asked one another question to the group, If you were Arjuna than How will you measure your progress, I learned the SMART framework that evening.

Ramdas responded, " I will track how many times I hit the bullseye out of ten attempts each day," there was a counter question from Guru Ji, "Is it Achievable?"

With daily practice and training, I believe I can achieve it, Ramdas sounded confident this time.

Next question from Guru Ji, Ramdas, Is it Relevant to your overall ambition of being the best archer? Ramdas with a loud voice- "Absolutely"

And what is your time-bound target? Guru Ji questioned.

If I am Arjuna and Donacharya is my coach then "I will achieve this within six months." Ramdas almost declared

Guru Ji appreciated Ramdas and people clapped in appreciation to Ramdas I learned you must have a SMART framework- Specific Measurable, Achievable, Realistic, and Time-bound

Now, let's break down your goal into smaller, manageable steps. In the case of archery, Guru Dronacharya taught Arjuna to work on his stance and, second, perfect his grip. Third focus on his aim, and lastly practice daily with dedication.

He became a master archer because he followed this step-by-step plan meticulously. Arjuna worked on each aspect of his archery.

I attended a very interesting and educational session. Ramdas asked his Guru Ji, "Would Arjuna have become the master archer without facing any obstacles or failure?" The interactions taught me that "Obstacles are part of the journey." No matter how dedicated you are, there will be moments of frustration and self-doubt. I also remember asking my father for advice on how to handle such situations, and his answer was simple: "Stay focused on your goal, keep learning new techniques, and keep practicing."

Years later, while working as a senior leader in the industry, I realized the importance of aligning goals with values. I always used to ask my team members, "Why do you want to be the best salesperson?" They had various responses, such as wanting to bring honor to their family. I would encourage them by saying, "Let your dedication and hard work reflect those values and your commitment to achieving it will be unwavering."

Key Takeaway Messages from this story:

1- Clarity and Specificity

2- SMART Goals

3- Step-by-Step Planning

4- Overcoming obstacles

5- Aligning goals with Values

Exercise

1- What specific actions can you take today to start moving towards your goal, and how will you ensure you consistently perform these actions?

2- Reflect on a time when you had the knowledge to achieve something but didn't follow through. What prevented you from taking action?

3- How can you overcome similar obstacles in the future?

4- What measurable milestones, can you set to track your progress toward your goal, and how will you hold yourself accountable for reaching each milestone?

How to Set Goals?

Everyone understands the importance of goal setting, still, some don't plan and a few plans, but don't follow the process and fail. At the same time, there are many leaders who follow the process and achieve greater success in their lives. I wish you were one among them,

Goals are important so plan well and achieve them. A goal-setting process helps you to focus on the journey, not just the end destination.

Remember the famous saying, "Those who focus only on the journey miss the adventure of the journey," Embracing the journey is where growth and learning happen.

I would suggest these simple steps that will help you to set SMART goals-

1. Always Start with Small Steps; First identify that one small task you can do today. This step must move you closer to your goal, for example- your goal is to improve your fitness. Then what can be one small step? Daily walking can be one small step so start with 1000 steps walk. Consistency and discipline are important elements for success so schedule this small task into your daily routine, Go for a walk at a specific time each day to ensure consistency. Daily tracking will bring discipline to your routine.

2. Use Learning from Past Mistakes; Reflect on a past goal you didn't achieve. Write down on a sheet of paper and be honest to yourself. Find out what went wrong and what obstacles you faced. Write at least one strategy against each obstacle. I have seen a major reason why people fail is Procrastination. If your issue was procrastination as well then plan specific times for working on tasks and eliminate distractions during those periods.

3. Set Milestones; Break down your major or main goal into smaller, manageable milestones. Review the progress regularly. For example, your goal is to write a book in the next 90 days, then set milestones for completing each chapter. Set weekly or monthly check-ins to assess your progress towards each milestone and make adjustments if necessary.

Remember: By planning your steps and focusing on the journey, you will enjoy the adventure and be better equipped this time to achieve your goals.

Let us recap our learnings-

Setting SMART goals is your blueprint for success.

We explored the critical role of goal-setting in achieving success, both personally and professionally.

Goals provide direction, motivation, and a clear roadmap for where you want to go and how to get there.

Clear and specific goals are essential.

SMART framework- SMART stands for Specific, Measurable, Achievable, Relevant, and Time-bound. This framework helps ensure that your goals are well-defined and attainable within a specific time frame. It is easier to track progress and stay focused.

We understood the process of goal setting. We also learned that Goal setting is not just about identifying end results but also about planning the steps needed to achieve those results. We also learned why is it important to break down larger goals into smaller and manageable tasks. It help to achieve it fast.

We discussed common obstacles to achieving goals. For example, Procrastination, lack of resources, and fear of failure. We also discussed about overcoming these challenges by developing strategies to overcome them.

We discussed why aligning your goals with your core values is important. It creates a sense of purpose and fulfillment.

Stories provided practical insights and inspiration, demonstrating the transformative power of setting and pursuing meaningful goals.

Key takeaways

Clarity and Specificity: Easy to pursue and measure

SMART Goals: use the SMART framework to create effective and achievable goals.

Break down goals into smaller tasks: it is easy to manage.

Overcoming Obstacles: Identify potential challenges and develop strategies to address them.

Alignment of Values: ensure your goals align with your long-term vision and core values for sustained motivation.

"Implement these principles to set yourself up for success and make significant strides toward achieving your aspirations".

Remember: Goal setting is not just a one-time activity but an ongoing process that requires commitment, adaptability, and continuous effort.

Setting SMART goals is a powerful tool for achieving your vision. It is a solid foundation for success. Please keep in mind that even the most meticulously planned goals can encounter obstacles and setbacks. There may be reasons beyond your control, you may suffer setbacks. This is where the mindset you bring to your goals becomes crucial.

While SMART goals give you a clear roadmap for success, it's your mindset that will keep you on the path, especially when you face a challenge. People with a growth mindset always see these obstacles as opportunities for growth and success. Learn from each setback and keep moving to achieve your goals. We will discuss a growth mindset in detail in our next chapter.

Developing a Growth Mindset

I want to share a scenario with you. Imagine setting a SMART goal to increase your sales by 15% this year and taking all the necessary steps as per the set process. Everything goes well in the first quarter, with sales growth matching your plan. However, in the next quarter, a price disruption made by your competitor makes your goal harder to reach. This is where the importance of a growth mindset comes into play and becomes crucial.

Remember: A growth mindset is your belief. You can develop a growth mindset through your dedication and hard work.

I suggest you take the following key actions to develop a Growth Mindset:

Embrace Challenges: accept obstacles as opportunities for growth rather than threats. Move out of your comfort zone, a new challenge is waiting for you to tackle. Push your boundaries and learn a new skill or develop new skills.

Learn from feedback: Invite feedback from your colleagues, friends, and team members. Even if you get constructive criticism accept it for your improvement. Use this feedback as a tool to identify areas for growth and make necessary adjustments.

Persist in the face of setbacks: Resilience is key to a growth mindset. Setbacks are part of your journey, treat them like a halt or small station, pass that station with a smile, and continue progressing toward your goals.

These simple actions can help you cultivate a growth mindset, making you a winner no matter how challenging the situation.

Storytime

I invite you to join me to have fun learning to ride a bicycle. I believe your experience is no different than mine. My excitement was matching the shiny new bike with my old bicycle. There was a different world of balancing on two wheels. For many of us, this experience was a turning point in our childhood, filled with falls, scrapes, and unwavering encouragement from those around us.

Ramdas always used to share the knowledge he gained from his Guru Ji (Sage). He was a great learner and a skilled trainer. He often compared life's challenges to learning how to ride a bicycle, making difficult situations seem simple for others to overcome.

He used to say, "Success is like riding a bicycle. At first, you're bound to fall, but with each fall, you learn something new." One day, I (A young boy) decided to master bicycling. I took a challenge to ride my bicycle around the village without stopping. My Village had no proper road in those days so it was a little more challenging task. The first few steps were tough and failed in the first many attempts. I lost balance and fell countless times. Honestly telling each fall was painful and tempted me to give up. But with every fall I got a solid backup, determined to try again.

Ramdas noticed my struggle and shared some wisdom with me. He said, "Setting a goal is the first step, but maintaining the right midset will help me achieve it. Every time you fall, you learn how to balance better. Each scrap and bruise is a lesson in disguise."

With renewed determination, I practiced every day. I embraced the challenge, learned from each mistake, and persisted despite the setbacks. I remember that on the 14th day after my first fall, I was able to ride my bicycle around my village without stopping and without falling. "A scar on my right leg is a mark of my 1st win."

The confidence I gained that day is with me even today as it was along the way.

This story of my learning to ride a bicycle is not just about achieving a childhood goal. It's about the importance of setting clear goals and developing a growth mindset .

When we set SMART goals, we are laying out a clear path to success. However, it is our perseverance, our ability to learn from failures, and our willingness to tackle challenges that ultimately drive us to achieve our ambitions.

Remember: Every goal you set is similar to learning how to ride a bicycle. It will require effort, patience, and resilience. With the right mindset, you can achieve anything you set your mind to.

Why is Growth Midset Crucial for Success?

A growth mindset is crucial for success because it fosters continuous improvement, resilience, and adaptability. Let me share a few points with you about keeping sales leaders in the centre.

Embracing Challenges

If you are working in sales then you are experiencing that the sales landscape is dynamic, with constantly changing markets , preferences of customers are changing very fast and so is the competition growing.

How a growth mindset will help in these situations?

Sales leaders with a growth mindset always view challenges as opportunities for learning and growth. These leaders take on difficult tasks and innovate to meet new demands.

These leaders learn from the feedback they receive from their customers, peers, and seniors and they use this feedback to improve their sales process. They are open to constructive criticism as well, they use this valuable information to refine their approach which makes them a better sales leader.

Have you noticed that rejection and setbacks are very common in sales. If you are in process of building your sales career or planning for a successful sales journey then accept this fact; "Not every sales pitch will be successful and not every deal will close."

A growth mindset instills resilience that allows you to bounce back from disappointments. Leaders with a growth mindset understand that failure is a part of the learning process. They remain motivated to keep trying until they succeed.

Technology is evolving rapidly, with new tools and methods being introduced every day. To stay relevant in a competitive market, it's important to cultivate a growth mindset and be open to experimenting with new techniques to enhance your sales processes.

Effective leadership involves not only personal success but also the growth and development of team members. You need to lead from the front and create an atmosphere of continuous learning and improvement. This approach will foster a culture of growth and high performance within the organization.

Leaders with a growth mindset have a long-term vision and set their goals accordingly. They know achieving long-term success requires setting ambitious yet achievable goals and maintaining focus over time.

Remember: set and pursue long-term goals with a clear vision.

My suggestion: Remain dedicated to your goals and exert the necessary effort to overcome obstacles and achieve success.

Here are a few practical tips to help you develop a growth mindset:

Don't avoid difficult clients; in the beginning, you will find interaction difficult but each such experience will become a chance to refine your approach and develop new strategies.

Don't ignore any feedback: Rather seek feedback from your clients and peers. Use constructive criticism as a tool for growth. This will help you build stronger relationships with your customers.

Every 'NO' will take you closer to a 'Yes'. So remain persistent.

Invest time with customers to understand their behavior better, and use technologies and adapt to new methods to improve your sales pitch.

"A growth mindset will transform you into resilient, adaptable, and continuously improving professionals who can lead their teams to sustained success."

There are many examples of leaders with a growth mindset. For example

Larry Page- co-founder of Google

Larry Page is the epitome of a leader with a growth mindset. He has demonstrated how relentless pursuit of learning and innovation can lead to monumental success. In 1998, Larry Page and his colleague Sergey Brin founded Google while they were still Ph.D. students. Despite the challenges of establishing a new company in a market with established search engines, Page persisted due to his growth mindset. One of Page's key strengths was his refusal to accept the status quo.

He saw every challenge as an opportunity to learn and innovate. Page and Brin's development of the PageRank algorithm revolutionized search technology by ranking web pages based on their relevance and importance.

Page invited feedback and worked on that feedback to improve their search engine.

His growth mindset can be best exemplified by his continuous drive for innovation and results are-

Google Maps, Gmail, Android, and even self-driving cars by its subsidiary Waymo.

Cultivating and Nurturing high-performing teams

Page understood the importance of nurturing a culture of growth within Google. He was always encouraging his people to 'think big and take risks'.

Example - "20% time" policy, which allowed employees to spend 20% of their time working on projects they were passionate about.

Result; Products like "Gmail and Adsense"

The key takeaway from Larry Page's story-

Embrace Challenges

Learn from Feedback

Persist through setbacks

Innovate continuously

Remember-'"A growth mindset has the power to not only transform an individual, but also an entire industry."

There are numerous examples of a few leaders who are renowned for their growth mindset. For example-

Sheryl Sandberg-COO of Facebook

Elon Musk-CEO of SpaceX and Tesla. Ground-breaking advancements in space travel and electric vehicles.

Jeff Bezos- Founder of Amazon: transformed his company from an online book store to a global e-commerce and cloud compounding giant.

Satya Nadela- CEO of Microsoft. Revitalized the company by fostering a culture of learning and innovation.

Indira Nooyi- Former CEO of PepsiCo – The company transformed its product portfolio by incorporating healthier options and expanding its global reach.

Summary

So far, we've discussed the importance of embracing a growth mindset, particularly for sales leaders. A growth mindset is the belief that abilities and intelligence can be developed through dedication, hard work, and perseverance. Now, let's focus on learning sales techniques to become a superstar in your career.

EFFECTIVE SALES STRATEGIES

"Selling is not about convincing people to buy, it's about finding the right solution to a problem they have."

- Zig Ziglar

Let me share the experience of one of my participants here, This might be the case with you as well. and his experience should help you to have a better understanding of, sales, selling, and sales techniques that will make you a star salesperson and an effective leader.

In the early stages of my career, I sought to understand the concept of sales. Many individuals offered their insights, but their varying perspectives only left me more perplexed. Some defined sales as "the exchange of a commodity for money," While others argued that it encompasses "any activity that involves transferring the ownership of a good or commodity to the buyer in exchange for a monetary price." Even after consulting books, I found myself further confounded. According to one book, sales is defined as the set of activities a business undertakes to facilitate customers' purchases of their product."

I was confused when I read about a transaction, which is a transition between two or more parties where the buyer receives the goods or services in exchange for a certain amount of money. I asked my mentor if the money paid to the seller is called a sale. His response was more elaborate as he explained to me, "Sales refers to the activities and processes you adopt in promoting and selling goods or services." He talked about sales strategies and different methods. Later, I realized the importance of these methods.

I was convinced by the words of my mentor, but still was not fully clear about my question, What is Sales? I was not selling any goods, I was promoting my products to a customer who was not a buyer himself but was a prescriber to his customers.

I read more about Sales attended a few seminars and got more clarity for myself.

I liked the statement of Shiv Khera, a well-known motivational speaker and author, who said, "Sales is 90% conviction of a salesperson and 10% is communication of his conviction."

This insight highlights the importance of belief in the product and the ability to effectively communicate that belief.

Let me ask you a question, Have you visited a smartphone store to buy a new handset with the latest features? Can you think of a salesperson who genuinely believes in the cutting-edge features and reliability of a new smartphone? His passion, his confidence, and his knowledge of how the phone's advanced camera and extended battery life can enhance your daily life. You have that smartphone in your hand now. Not ask yourself, have you purchased a new smartphone or the confidence of the salesperson? That is the conviction of a salesperson.

Another example could be of a real estate agent who is fully convinced that a particular property offers unmatched value. Their enthusiasm is contagious as they describe the property's unique features, such as its prime location and modern amenities, making it easier for potential buyers to see the value and make a purchase decision.

Sometimes people confuse Sales with Selling. As you know Sales is an outcome and selling is a process. Selling is a process of persuasion that encourages a prospect to take action.

Sometimes sales happen without selling. Do you agree?

Let me share one of my experience that helped me to learn about sales. Please join me to visit the memory lane of my childhood.

Storytime

One day, Ramdas shared an experience with his "Guru Ji," The Saga) he began, "I recently bought a shirt for an important occasion. It was quite expensive, and I had no choice since the market was closed and only one shop was open."

Guru Ji listened intently and then posed a thought-provoking question, Ramdas, did you buy a shirt or did you buy a solution to your problem?

Ramdas was puzzled, "I don't understand, Guru Ji," he replied.

Guru JI with a familiar smile on his face explained that People are rarely interested in a product or service itself; they are interested in how it can solve their problems. In your case, the problem was needing a shirt for the occasion, and the solution was finding one in the only open shop The shirt was secondary to the need it fulfilled.

Ramdas pondered this and began to see the deeper lesson. Guru Ji continued, "Effective Sales strategies are not about pushing products onto people." Let me ask you this, Ramdas: if the market had been open, would you have bought the same shirt at that price, or would you have explored other options for a better shirt at a more economical price?"

Ramdas thought for a moment and responded, "I would have definitely explored the options to find a better shirt at a lower price."

As a small boy, I was learning new things and was more curious to understand the Psychology of sales. I asked Ramdas, given a chance would you like to visit that shop again?

You can guess his answer. It was No. Rightly so, the salesperson has taken advantage of the situation and lost the opportunity to build trust.

Guru Ji nodded. "Exactly. When given choices, people will always seek the best solution to their problems. If a salesperson merely pushes a product without understanding the customer's needs, they miss the opportunity to offer the best solution. The goal should always be to align the product or service with the customer's specific needs and preferences."

I learned a valuable lesson that day, which has been incredibly beneficial in my sales career.

My key takeaway on that day was:

1. Always start by identifying the specific needs of the customers.

2. Provide a Solution, Not just a product.

3. Offer choices- whenever possible offer customers a variety of options. This empowers them to make the best decision and feel more satisfied with their purchase.

4. Build Trust through understanding. It is easy if you genuinely understand the needs of the customers and help them in making the best decision.

5. Focus on Value and not on Price- Emphasize the values and benefits of your product rather than just its price. Show how it provides a better solution compared to alternatives.

Effective Sales Strategies are not about pushing products onto people but about understanding and meeting their needs, offering them choices, and ensuring they feel they have made the best decision.

We will talk about the importance of customer-focused sales techniques that have stood the test of time and are essential for achieving success in sales. These techniques will help you and your teams to connect with customers, understand their needs, and close deals effectively and will make your team a performing team.

A. Consultative Selling

Consultative selling is a sales approach that is very effective and useful to build relationships with customers and understand their needs, challenges, and goals. This approach is not about pushing a product or service, the salesperson acts as an advisor or consultant and offers tailored solutions that specifically address the customer's unique situation. Each customer is different and so are their needs, and challenges. By practicing this approach, a salesperson becomes a trusted advisor or consultant. Let me share some pillars or we can say fundamental aspects of consultative selling.

Fundamental Aspects of Consultative Selling:

Please ensure that you have in-depth knowledge about the industry you are dealing with.

1. Know Your Customer Well: Before planning the sales interaction with the customer, conduct research to gather more information about their business and specific pain points.

2. Be a good listener: When you are with your customer and during the conversation, pay close attention to what the customer says. This will help you understand his current situation. By asking open-ended questions you can uncover their true needs and challenges. You will agree that active listening is more than just hearing words; it's about fully engaging with your customer,

understanding their needs, and showing empathy. This technique involves listening to understand, rather than listening to respond.

I suggest one effective way to practice active listening- "asking open-ended questions" Open-ended questions can not be answered with a simple "yes" or "no." In fact these questions will encourage your customers to share more detailed information and provide a better understanding of their needs and challenges.

Let me share one example: "Imagine you are a sales representative for a software company." You have a meeting with a potential client, There are two options to start the meeting,

a- Are you happy with your current software?

b- Can you tell me about the challenges you're currently facing with your existing software system?

Which one will give you more time to understand the needs of your client? Of course option " b" will encourage the client to elaborate on their experiences and pain points. This will help you to demonstrate that you are genuinely interested in their situation, whereas option "a" may lead to a short and uninformative answer.

3. Building Trust and Relationships: you can build long-lasting relationships with your customers by showing genuine concern for their problems and demonstrate a willingness to help solve them. You establish your

expertise and reliability through knowledge, experience, and honesty.

4. Provide Tailored Solutions: A proper analysis of the customer's need and how your product or service can meet their needs will help you to provide a solution. This approach will help you develop a solution that is specifically designed to address the customer's unique requirements.

5. Role of an Advisor: To educate your customers, you should have better knowledge about industry trends, and best practices. With your industry knowledge and understanding of the challenges faced by your customers, you can offer advice and insights that help the customer make informed decisions. This will make you a trusted advisor rather than just a salesperson.

Long-Term Perspective: Always prioritize building long-term relationships over one-time sales. After the sale, continue to support customers, ensuring satisfaction and providing assistance with their challenges.

Let me share one example of becoming a Trusted Advisor in the Pharmaceutical Industry.

One of my friends a sales superstar in his organization, shared his experience with a leading consultant in the town. It was the launch of a new diabetes brand to the consultant who was an endocrinologist by qualification and treated patients with diabetes. My friend did his research on Dr's specific challenges and needs.

I requested my friend to share his conversation with Dr Rajesh (Leading Consultant). Enjoy the conversation- I will use Me for my friend and Dr Rajesh for his customer.

Me- Dr. Rajesh, can you tell me about the biggest challenges you face when managing your patient's diabetes?

Dr Rajesh's Response- One of the biggest issues is ensuring that my patients adhere to their medication schedules. Many of them find it difficult to manage their blood sugar levels effectively.

Me- I understand how challenging adherence can be. What strategies have you found effective so far, and where do you feel there are still gaps?

Dr Rajesh's response- We have tried various patient education programs and reminder systems, but many patients still struggle, especially those with complicated schedules.

Me- (I was listening to Dr Rajesh carefully and was showing my genuine interest in Dr Rajesh) based on my conversation I made my points and potential solutions.

I continued- Our new medication has a simpler dosing regimen, which can significantly help with adherence. Additionally, we offer a patient support program that includes educational material and digital reminders tailored to each patient's need. I shared clinical trials and experiences of his colleagues in different cities.

Dr Rajesh, that sounds Good, let us develop a plan.

Me- I understood the need of Dr Rajesh and instead of pushing my brand I suggested – How about we start with a small group of patients who struggle the most with adherence? We can monitor the progress closely and adjust our approach based on the results.

Outcome: I focused on Dr Rajesh's challenges and provided a tailored solution, I positioned myself as a trusted advisor. My approach was simple and offered practical support that addressed the patient's needs.

If you work in the pharmaceutical industry, you can assist your team members in becoming trusted advisors, leading to stronger client relationships and improved patient outcomes.

Takeaway from the above conversation:

Engage Fully- practice active listening by giving your full attention to the customer.

Ask Open-Ended Question

Show Empathy-Demonstrate that you understand and care about the client's needs.

Tailor Your Solutions- Use the information gathered to offer solutions that specifically address the customer's challenges

Build Trust- Active listening helps build a stronger relationship with the customer, fostering trust and credibility.

Collaborate and implement – Work with your customers to develop a plan that integrates your solution seamlessly into their existing practices.

B. Spin Selling

SPIN Selling was developed by Neil Rackham, a renowned psychologist and founder of Huthwaite International. His efforts and research in the late 1980s revolutionized the sales industry by shifting the focus from traditional sales tactics to a more consultative approach. Reckham's influential sales technique emphasizes understanding the customer's needs and guiding them through a decision-making process using a series of strategic questions. His work has had a profound impact on sales training and is widely used by sales professionals across various industries to achieve better results.

Let us understand SPIN Technique in detail, which is structured around four types of questions: Spin selling is a consultative sales technique that helps you build strong relationships with customers by focusing on their needs and problems.

- **A-** Situation Questions: To understand the customer's current situation. For example – a Pharma Sales Representative might ask his customer (a Doctor), Which are your choices about the current medications you prescribe for diabetes?

B- Problem Questions: These questions are designed to understand the challenges customers face, including difficulties with current diabetes treatment options.

C- Implication Questions: To understand, "What could be the effect of a problem on the customers they are facing." For example- How does the difficulty in managing patient adherence affect their overall health outcomes?

D- Need-Payoff Questions: These questions help the customer understand the value of a solution and how it addresses their needs. For example- would a medication with a simpler dosing regimen help improve your patient adherence and health outcomes?

This technique is similar to the 5th habit from "The Seven Habits of Highly Successful People" By Steven Covey. This habit says- Seek first to understand then to be understood."

Asking appropriate questions may not come easily to most people, but with determination, one can gain mastery in this technique. "Spin Selling" recommends developing a questioning mindset, emphasizing that it's more important to understand than to immediately respond.

Appropriate questions- questions that are relevant, thoughtful, and effectively aligned with the context or goal of the conversation. In the sales context, appropriate questions are designed to :

1- Gather Information- Help you in understanding your customer's current situation and needs.

2- Identify Problems- What are the challenges and issues of your customers?

3- Explore Implications: Delve into the consequences of the customer's problems.

4- Highlight Needs and Benefits: help the customer in recognizing the value of potential solutions.

Let me share that there is no right or wrong question, it is the situation or context that makes it right or wrong so focus on asking appropriate questions for example-

How many team members are involved in the decision-making process?

Can you please describe your current process for managing inventory?

These questions are fact-finding questions and you can establish context.

A few examples of problem questions –

What difficulties are you experiencing with your current supplier?

Are there any challenges you have encountered with product reliability?

You can think and design implication questions and need payoff questions.

Let me discuss about the importance of asking appropriate questions:

Builds Trust: Demonstrates that you are genuinely interested in understanding and solving the customer's problem.

Gathers Crucial Information: Provides insights needed to tailor your solution to the customer's specific needs.

Guides the Conversation: This helps you to lead the conversation towards areas where your product or service can provide the most value.

Engages Customers: Encourages the customer to think critically about their needs and the potential benefits of your solution.

Remember: "By asking appropriate questions, you can effectively uncover customer needs, build stronger relationships, and position your products or services as the ideal solution."

C. Value Selling

Value selling focuses on demonstrating the value your product or service brings to the customer. This technique helps you to understand what the customer values most and you can align your product's benefits with those values. To be effective in this technique you need to;

- Identify the key benefits of your product.
- Understand what the customer values most, for some, it may be cost-saving, and for some efficiency, and for others it can be quality.

- Tailor your sales pitch to highlight how your product meets those values.

Let me explain this with an example of an IT Industry: Software as a service

This company offers project management software designed to streamline workflows and enhance collaboration. The sales executive, Shilpi, is engaging with a potential client, a mid-sized marketing agency.

Shilpi with her homework and list of questions in her mind reached the client's office to understand the client's needs.

If you were Shilpi, then your first question could be -

Can you share some of the biggest challenges your team faces with your current project management system?

Listen to your customer carefully, and show genuine interest in their challenges and pain areas.

The response from Shilpi's client was that our system is outdated and does not integrate well with other tools we use, leading to inefficiencies and missed deadlines.

Imagine yourself in this situation and you can align the features of the project management software with the client's needs, focusing on the value and benefits rather than just the feature.

Let us see Shilpi's response- I understand your problem, and I would like to share that our software seamlessly integrates with your existing tools like Slack and Google Drive, which will streamline your workflows and ensure your team meets deadlines. Just for example, our client ABC Marketing saw a 30% increase in project completion rates within the first months of using our software.

Did you notice how Priya provides a tangible example of how the software has benefitted similar clients?

She explained further- By reducing the time spent on manual updates and improving team collaboration, our clients typically save about 10 hours per week. This translates to significant cost savings and allows your team to focus on more strategic initiatives.

This is a proven technique that your team can easily learn and implement to achieve the desired results for the organization.

D. Social Selling

Social selling leverages social media platforms to connect with potential customers, build relationships, and engage with prospects.

You can take simple steps to improve the visibility of your brand and reach more number of customers within no time. I suggest to take the following steps-

- To build strong online platforms like LinkedIn, X, Facebook, and Medium, Share valuable content and insights relevant to your industry.

- To engage with prospects by commenting on their posts, sharing their content, and starting a conversation.

Recently I saw a post on my LinkedIn page from Zaara, a real estate agent stating that I have expertise in the local market and helping home buyers by providing home-buying tips, and virtual tours of new listings. I found her message activity engaging and I feel this is a perfect example of social selling.

The message on my page was- Hi, JP, I noticed you liked my post about the best neighborhoods for families. If you are considering a move, I would love to help you find the perfect home. Let me know more about what you're looking for, so I can provide you with relevant information.

Do you think, she was trying to establish that she is a knowledgeable and approachable real estate agent, building trust and growing her connections list?

We have seen that these techniques are useful across the industry.

Let us see a few more w techniques –

E. Relationship Selling

This technique emphasizes building long-term relationships with customers and not focusing on immediate sales. Relationship-Selling is about developing trust and loyalty over time.

Suggested actions;

- Focus on building rapport and trust with customers
- Provide exceptional customer service and follow-up after-sales
- Stay in touch with customers and nurture the relationship over time.

F. Cross-Selling and Upselling

Cross-selling involves offering complementary services while upselling encourages customers to purchase a higher-end product or add-on feature.

Suggested actions;

- Identify opportunities for cross-selling and upselling during the sales process.
- Highlight the benefits of additional products or upgraded features.
- Ensure that the additional offerings genuinely add value to the customers.

Let me share two examples of cross-selling for better understanding.

1. Imagine you are purchasing a new laptop from an online electronic store.

The website suggests related products such as a laptop bag, an external mouse, and a laptop cooling pad. You start thinking of scorching heat and high temp and feel that the cooling pad will surely add value to your purchase.

Now that you have purchased a laptop bag and cooling pad, you decided to look for a stylish laptop bag to give your laptop a different experience and keep it safe, while also enhancing its look. Suddenly, a pop-up appears on your screen offering a high-precision external mouse at a very attractive price, just as you're making payments for the laptop and these accessories.

2-Banking – I am sure you have this experience yourself. You have opened a savings account with your bank and the bank employee suggests additional financial products like a recurring account with a higher interest rate, and also our credit card comes with a cashback reward that could benefit you. Would you like more information on these products? He assures you that a bank representative will come and explain the benefits to you at your place.

Upselling example;

Have you been to a restaurant or a coffee café recently? You might have experienced the following yourself and can be a perfect example of Upselling.

You order a regular coffee and

The executive there suggests upgrading to a larger size for a small additional cost. With a smile on her face, says- Sir, would you like to upgrade to a large coffee for just 50 cents more? You will get more of your favourite brew with your favorite flavour to enjoy!

Another experience can be at an E-Commerce website during the purchase of a smartphone.

You are searching for a basic model and the website highlights a higher-end model with additional features such as a better camera and more storage capacity.

You see a message on your screen reading as- "For just $100 more, you can upgrade to our premium model which includes a super camera and double the storage. Take your smartphone experience to the next level!" In most of cases, you have taken your smartphone experience to the next level.

Summary

In this chapter, we explored various effective sales techniques essential for driving success in the competitive world of sales.

Key takeaway

1- Consultative Selling: This approach focuses on understanding the customer's needs and providing tailored solutions. By asking appropriate questions and actively listening, you can build strong relationships and become trusted advisors.

2- SPIN Selling: Developed by Neil Rackham, spin selling involves asking Situation, Problem, Implication, and Need-Payoff questions to uncover customer needs and demonstrate the value of the solution. This method emphasizes the importance of understanding the customer's context and challenges.

3- Value Selling: This technique emphasizes the unique value and benefits of a product or service, rather than just its features. By clearly communicating how a solution addresses specific customer pain points, you can differentiate your offerings.

4- Social Selling: Leveraging social media platforms to engage with potential customers, share valuable content, and build relationships Social selling involves creating a professional online presence and using networks to identify and connect with prospects.

5- Cross-Selling and Upselling: Cross-selling involves recommending related products or services, while upselling encourages customers to purchase higher-end versions or additional features.

These techniques help maximize the value of each customer interaction and increase overall sales.

To be successful practice the following:

1- Understand and address customer needs.

2- Communicate value effectively.

3- Leverage social media

4- Maximize sales opportunities

5- Build strong and long-term relationships.

By mastering these proven sales techniques, you can enhance your sales effectiveness, build stronger relationships with customers, and achieve greater success in your sales career.

Remember: "The key to successful selling is to understand your customer's needs, provide valuable solutions, and maintain a customer-centric approach throughout the sales process."

We now understand that the foundation of successful selling lies in the strategies and methods we employ. However, even the most powerful techniques can fall short without the support of a dedicated and capable team. Sales success is not just about individual effort but about the collective strength and synergy of the entire team. In the next chapter, we will discuss the essential elements of creating a winning sales team. You as a leader have the power so focus on team dynamics, leadership, and fostering a culture if excellence, you can transform individual potential into outstanding team performance.

I invite you to join me to explore how to build and nurture a high-performing sales team that drives sustained success.

Building a High-Performing Sales Team

"Individually, we are one drop, together we are an ocean."

*- **Ryunosuke Satoro***

Let us shift our focus from individual sales skills to team dynamics and performance. This transition will be very helpful in the comprehensive exploration of how to build, lead, and maintain an effective sales team. An effective team means guaranteed sustained success.

In this chapter, we will focus on the importance of a high-performing team. The elements of building such a team and the role of a leader. You have a major role to play and it starts from the right recruitment, the right training, setting clear goals and your expectations from team, the right motivation, and then your role in team success.

Let us travel together-

Importance of A High-Performing Team

Henry Ford once said, "Coming together is a beginning, keeping together is progress. Working together is a success." This quote perfectly encapsulates the essence of building and leading a high-performing team. Ramdas, our guide in all previous episodes and the central character in the Rise and

Thrive Series has lived these values and followed the same process from the formation of a team to team success.

Storytime

Ramdas, a very talented person stood out as a natural leader. He was the captain of the football team and the unopposed leader for all significant events. I can with pride, that his charisma, dedication, and ability to inspire others made him a beloved figure and favorite to his Guru Ji and me personally. We used to have an annual function every year and that particular year our village head decided to organize a grand fair, a tradition that brought joy and unity to the community. Naturally, Ramdas was given the charge to form his team and organize the fair.

Though I was a small boy at that time I still remember his efforts. I suggest you be with me in this preparation and make your team that will be a high-performing team for sustained growth.

Ramdas shared with his Guru Ji that the success of the fair depended on having the right people. He carefully selected team members based on their skills and passion. For example, he chose my elder brother to handle logistics because he was known for his meticulous attention to detail. He requested his Guru Ji to suggest a name who has exceptional communication skills, this was an important role and the person was tasked with managing public relations and outreach. Ramdas was extremely talented and was able to recognize and harness the strength of his team members laying the foundation for a high-performing team.

Recruitment:

I still appreciate Ramdas and carry respect for his work with me every day. I am thankful for the valuable lesson he taught me. He didn't just look for people who could do the job, as shown in the above examples. He sought individuals who believed in the vision of creating an unforgettable event. He was certain that the team needed committed members for the event's success, and his approach ensured this. He only selected individuals committed to the overall task, not just their responsibilities.

Training:

After the team was formed, Ramdas organized a series of training sessions. He brought in experts from neighboring villages who had experience in organizing fairs. These experts taught the team how to set up stalls, manage crowds, and ensure safety. Every small point was explained to each team member. After that, Ramdas took over the center stage and led sessions on teamwork and communication, emphasizing the importance of working together seamlessly. The training not only equipped the team with the necessary skills but also built a strong sense of shared goals and trust among the members. My learning about how to communicate with team members, in a time when mobiles were not available, was very helpful during my sales journey.

Motivation:

Please remember Motivation is Motiv**e**+A**c**tion (read e and c as silent). Ramdas knew that motivation was key to maintaining high performance. He explained the motive of the team very clearly. I remember he held many meetings to discuss progress. He never missed any opportunity to appreciate the contribution of anyone. He was addressing challenges if it was faced by anyone in time. his enthusiasm was at its peak always and was able to inspire his team to achieve greater heights. His actions were simple but very powerful and a true motivation for his team. The best motivation I have seen in his team was the feeling of being valued.

Incentives:

Ramdas proposed a reward system and I still remember that system encouraged friendly competition and pushed everyone to give their best, for example- the person who managed to attract the most visitors to their stall would receive a special prize at the end of the fair.

Team Incentive was proposed by Ramdas, and I am sharing it with you to encourage you to plan the incentive for your team. Here are a few steps to make the incentive program effective;

1- Set Clear Criteria: This helps in maintaining transparency and fairness.

2- Communicate regularly: Keep the team informed about their progress towards earning incentives, Ramdas used weekly meeting as a platform, today you can send regular updates and use monthly review cum feedback sessions.

3- Encourage Team Spirit: Design incentives that promote collaboration rather than competition among team members.

4- Celebrate Wins: Never miss an opportunity to celebrate both small and big wins to keep the morale high and maintain a positive work environment.

Remember: "These incentive ideas can inspire your sales team to excel and achieve high performance. You can foster a culture of excellence within your team."

Feedback:

Ramdas was using weekly progress meetings to give feedback to team members. It was more on the strengths of individuals and also areas where they need to work more to be better in execution. This ensured that the team stayed aligned with its goals and there was no resistance from them to any changes or challenges.

Leadership in action:

Ramdas led by example. He was always the first to arrive and last to leave, working tirelessly alongside his team. His commitment and hard work inspired others to give their best. Ramdas was there to offer solutions and support. He created an environment where everyone felt empowered to contribute and take initiative.

Results:

The fair was a resounding success. The event went off without a hitch, and the entire village enjoyed a memorable day of fun and festivity. The team members felt a deep sense of pride and satisfaction in their accomplishments.

The experience taught us the value of teamwork, dedication, and effective leadership.

Everyone congratulated Ramdas for his planning and hard work. After a week or so Ramdas came to the village head and requested him to arrange some funds. The village head asked for the purpose and amount. His thought made the village head so happy and with the help of a few families he could arrange the same. Ramdas surprised everyone this time. he called for a post-event meeting and expressed his gratitude for their dedication. He then surprised them with the following-

"You have all worked tirelessly to make this fair a success. Your family has contributed significantly, so next Sunday will be a free day for all of you to relax and enjoy with your family. We (Ramdas, The Village Head, and his Guru Ji) are arranging food and small gifts for your family to show our appreciation for their support."

Every team member was thrilled by this announcement. They felt appreciated and valued, which was a great motivation for future projects.

Exercise

"Design an Incentive Plan for your Sales Team."

Creating a comprehensive incentive plan is essential for motivating your team and driving performance as a team leader. This exercise will guide you through designing both individual and team incentive plans that include monetary and non-monetary rewards.

Keep the following in mind while designing an Incentive Plan-

1- Understand your team's goal and preferences – write steps you would take to understand your team's motivations, and preferences.

2- Set clear and measurable objectives- Define the KPI that you will be using to measure success. Set SMART Goals (Specific, Measurable, Achievable, Realistic, and Time-Bound)

3- Design an incentive plan that includes separate components for individual and team incentives. (You can think of a Training Session or team-building workshop to improve skills and foster collaboration)

4- Communication plan- How will you communicate your plan to the team?

Let us summarize our learning from this chapter 'Creating a winning team':

1. Importance of High-Performing Teams- High-performing teams focus on shared goals and success. Stronger relationships are built within these teams, enhancing collaboration and productivity

2. Recruit Right; Right recruitment is the foundation of a high-performing team. Select individuals who not only have the necessary skills but also align with the team's values and culture.

3. Comprehensive Training- Equip team members with the skills and knowledge they need to excel in their roles.

4. Team Motivation- Motivation is key to sustaining high performance. Use a combination of monetary and non-monetary incentives to keep team members engaged and driven.

5. Setting Clear and SMART Goals- Ensure that these goals are in line with the organization's overarching objectives.

6. Communication- Foster an environment where team members feel comfortable sharing ideas and feedback. Open communication helps to identify and solve problems quickly and efficiently.

7. Reward and Recognition- Regularly acknowledge and reward the hard work and success of team members.

8. Feedback and course correction-Feedback should be actionable. Always give constructive feedback.

Remember: "Strong leadership is essential for guiding and inspiring the team, Leaders should lead by example, providing clear direction and support."

How can I get a competitive edge in this crowded market by using modern tools and data analytics to enhance my team's performance, and streamline processes? Are you having this question in your mind? If yes, then please join me here, in our next chapter we will focus on how sales leaders can use modern tools and data analytics to make my team more productive.

Leveraging Technology and Data in Sales

"Technology is best when it brings people together."

- Matt Mullenweg

In this chapter we will discuss the following;

Sales Technology and its importance

CRM System and how to choose the right CRM System and best practices of CRM Implementation

Decision-making based on Sales Analytics, the role of data in sales strategy, Key metrics, and KPIs to track

Sales automation tools

Digital sales platforms and E-commerce, strategies for effective selling, and tools for managing e-commerce sales

Tools for sales professionals

Continuous learning and development and future trends in Sales Technology.

Let us begin our journey to modernize our approach and stay ahead in a rapidly evolving sales landscape

In the past, we've found success in our sales careers by sticking to the fundamentals of sales management and traditional methods. However, today, technology isn't just an add-on; it's the foundation of modern sales strategies. There's a technological revolution taking place, and it's bringing about significant changes in the way sales teams operate.

As a sales leader, you should leverage these technologies to gain deeper insights into customer behavior, streamline your operations, and make data-driven decisions that propel your team toward success.

In today's highly competitive market, integrating technology into sales processes is not just an advantage; it's a necessity. We can't imagine life without the use of technology. Technology provides valuable insights, improves efficiency, and enables a more personalized customer experience.

Key aspects of sales technology and their importance:

A- Customer Relationship Management (CRM) System:

Today, it is widely used by companies for managing customer interactions, tracking sales activities, and storing customer information. The major benefits of using technology by sales teams are to stay organized and ensure that no lead of opportunity falls through the cracks.

Manually managing pipelines and tracking interactions is difficult for teams. Technology automates follow-up tasks, leading to increased productivity and improved customer relationships.

B- Sales Automation tools:

Automation tools streamline repetitive tasks such as sending emails, scheduling meetings, and data entry. This allows the representatives to focus more on building relationships and closing deals.

C- Data Analytics and Insights:

Such tools provide valuable information about customer behavior, and market trends. Data analytics tools also provide valuable insights into sales performance, which enable sales teams to make informed decisions, tailor their strategies, and predict future sales trends.

D- Artificial Intelligence(AI) and Machine Learning:

AI and machine learning can enhance various aspects of sales, from lead scoring and forecasting to personalized customer interactions. These technologies can analyze large datasets to predict customer needs and optimize sales pitches. Such tools provide predictive analytics and recommend the best times to contact leads, increasing the chances of conversion.

E- Social Selling Tools:

Social selling involves using social media platforms to connect with prospects and build relationships, Social tools help teams engage with leads, share valuable content, and establish themselves as expert in their industry.

F- Mobile Sales Solutions:

This is crucial for field sales teams and those who need to stay productive while traveling. You can perform some sales tasks on the go as well.

G- E-commerce and Online Sales Platforms:

These platforms facilitate online transactions, These platforms expand the reach of sales teams and provide an additional channel for revenue generation.

I suggest integrating these technologies into your sales strategies. You can boost productivity, enhance customer satisfaction, and gain a competitive edge. Effectively using technology in sales can revolutionize future growth and success.

Continuous Learning and Development in Sales Technology

The rapid pace if technology change requires to continually update your skills to stay relevant. However, time and resources for further education or training with work and personal commitments can be challenging. Sales technology is not static, it evolves to meet the changing needs of customers and businesses.

Here are a few suggestions in this context that will help you to have a competitive edge.

- a- Stay updated with new tools and technology- new tools are developed to improve efficiency and effectiveness. Attend webinars, and enroll in some online courses so you stay informed about new tools and best practices.

- b- On-Job Training and Skill Development-Continuous training ensures that sales teams are proficient in using current technologies and can adapt to new ones. On-job training can help sales teams keep their skills sharp and relevant.

- c- Embracing a culture of Learning- this kind of proactive approach can lead to innovative sales strategies and improved performance. Cultivating a culture that values continuous learning encourages team members to seek new knowledge and skills. I always recommend that sales leaders foster an environment of continuous improvement. Reward your team members for learning and applying new skills in their daily routines.

d- Invite Customer Feedback- This will help to get insights into shifting preferences and help sales teams adjust their approaches accordingly. As customer expectations evolve, so must the strategies and technologies used to meet them.

Leveraging Cross-Functional Knowledge- Encouraging cross-departmental training sessions and knowledge sharing can help sales teams gain broader perspectives and enhance their effectiveness. My coach organized such sessions once every quarter, and we all reaped the benefits. This allowed us to keep our teams updated with new technologies and methodologies, while also fostering team building.

Future Trends in Sales Technology

We must anticipate various trends that will influence the future of sales technology. Staying ahead of these trends is vital for maintaining a competitive edge.

Let me share a few –

a- Artificial Intelligence and Machine Learning- AI and Machine Leaning will provide deeper insights into customer behavior, enabling more precise targeting and tailored sales strategies.

b- Augmented and Virtual Reality- These apps enable customers to visualize products in their own environment, leading to more informed purchasing decisions..

c- Voice and Conversational AI- This will streamline communication and data entry, making the sales process more efficient and user-friendly.

d- Integration of Internet of Things – devices will provide real-time data and insights, enabling sales teams to offer more proactive and personalized solutions to customers.

e- Blockchain Technology- Can enhance transparency and security in transactions, fostering greater trust between buyers and sellers.

We can anticipate hyper-personalization where sales teams can create highly customized experiences for each customer. With the help of data analytics and AI, the sales team can generate solutions to meet the unique needs and preferences of each customer.

Remember: By embracing continuous learning and staying ahead of future trends, you can drive your teams to greater success. Encourage our teams to stay equipped with the latest tools and strategies to meet and exceed customer expectations.

Let us revisit our learning from sales technology and its importance.

1- embrace Continuous learning: Sales technology is continually evolving, and it is essential to stay updated with new tools and platforms. Maintaining a competitive edge requires a process of continuous learning.

2- Leverage Future Trends: emerging technology such as AI, Machine learning.AR/VR, Voice AI etc are set to revolutionize sales processes, so understand and prepare well.

3- Drive Efficiency and Effectiveness: be open to adopting new technology to stay ahead and have improved performance.

With a solid understanding of the latest sales technologies and their potential, let us focus on building and nurturing strong customer relationships. Technology is not just about making sales processes more efficient; it is also enhancing how we connect with and support our customers.

Strong customer relationships are crucial for driving loyalty and long-term success in sales.

Nurturing Customer Relationships

"Customer relationships are not built on sales transactions but on genuine connections and consistent value deliver."

- ***Unknown***

The heart of sales remains in the relationships we build with our customers. What does it take to build effective customer relationship management?

According to my interactions with my customers and my personal experience, it is the combination of the best of technology with the timeless principles of trust, empathy, and consistent engagement.

Remember- "Consistency is the key word"

Let us explore strategies to nurture and grow these relationships, ensuring that our customers remain at the center of our sales efforts.

Storytime

In an earlier chapter, I shared a story about my childhood memories of a fair and how Ramdas emerged as a natural leader and organized the event successfully. Now, let me share an episode at one of the stalls in the same fair, where Ramdas spent some time. The stall was about herbal remedies for general health.

Ramdas trained every member of the team to make a difference in their approach. He taught people a unique way of connecting with their customers. Every person who is visiting your stall should feel not only attended but also genuinely cared for.

One day the village head from my neighboring village visited this stall where Ramdas was advising the members. He heard a lot about herbal remedies and was eager to try them out for his chronic pain. Ramdas got a wonderful opportunity to demonstrate to the members how to connect with a customer and build relationships. Ramdas welcomed the head of the village warmly, offered a seat, and offered a cup of hot herbal tea. I along with my friends was watching the scene and were learning a new way. Ramdas initiated the discussion with inquiry about his life, family, his health concerns, and his goals for his village. The Village head felt comfortable and valued. Ramdas listened attentively, taking notes of his symptoms and concerns.

I thought that Ramdas would push his brand but to my surprise, Ramdas shared stories of other villagers who had similar issues and how they found relief. He provided information on ingredients and how they worked, making sure the visitor understood the value of each ingredient. The village head was feeling relieved and bought not just a product but a sense of trust and assurance.

Ramdas's approach teaches us an invaluable lesson about customer relationship management. It's not just about making a sale; it's about understanding your customers, addressing their needs, and building a lasting connection. This genuine care and attention turn customers into loyal advocates.

Months passed, and the village head's condition improved significantly. He became a regular customer and started referring others to Ramdas. What set Ramdas apart was not just the effectiveness of his herbs, but also the relationships he built. The village head regularly visited Ramdas to seek his advice on other conditions and to gather information about herbs, and every time he visited, he felt valued.

The essence of effective customer relationship management lies in creating meaningful interactions, providing consistent value, and maintaining a deep understanding of our customers' needs and aspirations.

Actionable insights from learning from Ramdas and the village head of my neighboring village.

1- **Understand your customers:** Effective customer relationship management starts with understanding your customers deeply. Listen to them attentively to know their needs, preferences, and feedback.

2- **Build Trust:** Ramdas did not just sell products; he educated village heads about the ingredients and their benefits.

3- **Follow-Up and Stay Engaged:** Regular follow-ups with your customers show that you value their relationship beyond the initial sale.

4- **Personalize Your Interactions:** Remember details about your customers to personalize your communication Address them by their names, nothing is closer than their names. Remember their preferences, and tailor your offers to meet their needs.

5- **Deliver Value Consistently:** Every customer is important and unique, so ensure every customer interaction is valuable. Always share useful information and add value with your advice.

These steps will help you to build strong, lasting relationships with your customers, just like Ramdas did.

Remember: These relationships are the foundation of sustained business success and customer loyalty.

Let us recap:

From this chapter on nurturing customer relationships, we learned that building and maintaining strong connections with your customers is crucial for long-term success. We must learn how to leverage these relationships for sustained growth and loyalty.

Let us explore how to effectively leverage customer feedback, analyze customer data, and utilize CRM tools to enhance your relationship management efforts further.

LEVERAGING TECHNOLOGY AND DATA FOR ENHANCED CUSTOMER INSIGHTS

"Without data, you're just another person with an opinion."

- W.Edwards Deming

In today's fast-paced, technology-driven world, successful leaders understand that using technology and data is no longer optional—it's essential. The ability to gather customer insights through advanced CRM systems and data analytics tools can mean the difference between merely maintaining customer relationships and turning them into powerful drivers of growth and loyalty.

Technology can provide a deeper understanding of customer behavior, preferences, and needs, ultimately driving more informed and strategic decision-making.

There is an abundance of data at your fingertips. Your ability to analyze and interpret this information is what will set you apart as a sales leader. Leveraging technology and data not only helps in understanding your customers better but also in anticipating their needs and exceeding their expectations.

We will explore various tools and techniques that can be employed to collect, analyze, and act upon customer data. Let us dive into the transformative power of technology and data in sales and how it can elevate your customer relationship management to unprecedented levels.

We will discuss with example the techniques and tools that you can use in your daily routine.

Pharma Marketing

Key Opinion Leader (KOL) engagement:

Identify the KOLs in your geography and collect information about them, Their opinion counts and they can help in building credibility and trust within the medical community.

You can use medical journals to provide more relevant and latest information about your brand. There are CRM tools available today that can help you to make well-informed decisions.

Digital Platforms: use digital platforms like Zoom, Google Meet, for patient education for their patients in managing their treatment and improving adherence. These platforms will also help them in educational sessions with healthcare professionals. These tools can also help in e-detailing and virtual sales calls. These tools enhance the reach and frequency of engagements.

If you are working in the FMCG sector:

Please remember the following text:

Remember to use platforms for trade promotion that assist with planning, executing, and analyzing trade promotions in order to increase sales. You can monitor progress on a daily basis and have real-time data to track improvements in productivity, product visibility, and sales volume in retail outlets.

Your sales team can gather and analyze consumer data to understand preferences and trends, this will help to identify the need to introduce new packs or new brands. They can inform product development teams to develop a new product and design new marketing strategies to be ahead of the competition.

There are tools and techniques available today to help manage customers and improve productivity in every sector.

Benefits: You can establish trust and cultivate long-term relationships with your customers, leading to improved business outcomes in the long run.

Key Takeaway message:

If you are in Pharma marketing-

Engage Key Opinion Leaders – build credibility and trust

Leverage E-detailing and Virtual Sales Calls.

In the FMCG Sales:

Implement Trade Promotions Management- Plan execute and analyze trade promotions to boost sales and product visibility in retail outlets with tools like SAP.

If you are in the Banking Sector:

Conduct Financial Needs Analysis- to assess the financial situation of clients and to offer tailored solutions and build long-term relationships.

We have been discussing different techniques and tools that can improve sales across various industries. It's important to remember that the key to successful sales strategies lies in building and maintaining strong customer relationships. Let's take a closer look at why nurturing these relationships is important and explore strategies for maintaining long-term customer loyalty.

Nurturing Customer Relationships

"Your most unhappy customers are your greatest source of learning."

- Bill Gates

Effective customer relationship management is the key to sustaining customer loyalty and driving long-term success.

Customer relationships are the bedrock of any successful business. Is it that easy? Can I achieve this by just providing a good product or service?

This is a long-term process that requires genuine engagement, empathy, and a commitment to understanding and meeting the evolving needs of your customers.

Storytime

In my hometown, there was a well-known bookstore owned by Mrs. Verma. She was a very soft-spoken and caring lady. As I began my career in sales, my father advised me to read more books on sales and self-improvement. I used to receive my salary on the 5th of each month, and it became a routine to visit Mrs. Verma's store to buy a book. She knew all her customers by name and remembered their favorite genres, and I was no exception. She would recommend books based on my previous purchases and always asked me for three action points from the last book I bought from her. This made me more mindful, and I started taking notes and preparing key action points from each book to implement in my life. This was her secret to exceptional customer relationships.

Whenever a customer walked in, Mrs. Verma's warm greeting and personalized suggestions made them feel valued and appreciated. I recall one incident where a new customer named Swati visited the store. She was looking for a specific book for her daughter's school project, which was out of stock. Mrs. Verma assured her that she would have the book ready by the next day. Not only did she keep her promise, but she also gifted Swati's daughter a bookmark and a small notebook as a gesture of goodwill.

Swati later became a regular customer after I recommended Mrs. Verma's store to her. She shared her positive experience with her family and friends. Mrs. Verma's dedication to nurturing customer relationships didn't just secure one sale; it built a community of loyal patrons who valued the personal touch they received at her bookstore.

I met Mrs. Verma with my friend at her bookstore after 25 years, and to my surprise, she called me by my first name. After exchanging pleasantries, she asked me about the last book I read and what my key action points were. I have such pleasant memories of Mrs. Verma, and I have a lot of love and respect for her approach and interest in her customers.

You can nurture customer relationships for long-term success by following the simple steps-

1- First Understand your customers:

Effective customer relationship management starts with understanding your customers deeply. Listen to them attentively to know their needs, preferences, and feedback.

2- Personalized your communication:

Use CRM tools to track customer preferences and purchase history to personalize communication and offers. Tailor your offers to meet their needs.

3- Build Trust:

Never try to push your product onto customers. Instead, focus on communicating the benefits of your product or service that meet their needs. Establish trust by being transparent and knowledgeable about your product, service, industry, and available options.

4- Follow-up and provide support:

Regular follow-up is a proactive service measure, so practice this, and provide support before customers even realize they need it. This proactive approach will improve overall customer satisfaction.

5- Feedback Mechanisms:

Create multiple channels for customers to provide feedback, such as direct communication, surveys, and social media. Actively listen to their concerns and suggestions and implement changes based on their input.

6- Deliver Value consistently:

Share useful information and add value with your advice to build long-lasting relationships.

7- Foster Customer Loyalty:

Have loyalty programs that offer rewards for regular customers, repeat purchases, and referrals. Create a sense of appreciation among your customers.

Remember: "Build strong, lasting customer relationships to drive sales and foster brand advocates."

Sometimes we get overburdened and so caught up in our daily routines that we miss out on some interesting moments in life and struggle to maintain a work-life balance.

Let us learn the importance of maintaining a balance that allows you to be at your best both professionally and personally.

Achieving Work-life Balance

"Work is a rubber ball. If you drop it, it will bounce back. The other four balls – family, health, friends, integrity- are made of glass. If you drop one of these, it will be irrevocably scuffed, nicked, perhaps even shattered."

– Gary Keller

Often, in the pursuit of professional success, personal well-being takes a back seat. However, achieving a harmonious balance between work and life is crucial for long-term success and happiness. Those who are unable to maintain this balance often feel stressed and burned out. This can erode the foundation of productivity and relationships, both at work and at home.

As a sales leader, your role demands constant attention and effort. It is vital to recognize the importance of maintaining a balance that allows you to be at your best both professionally and personally.

Together we will explore strategies to achieve a healthy work-life balance, ensuring sustained success and well-being.

How to strike the right balance? This is a common question people ask me during my interactions with them during productivity sessions. You might have this question in your mind.

Here are a few suggestions :

Learn to prioritize tasks:

Use tools like the Eisenhower Matrix, also known as the Urgent and Important Matrix.

Learn to distinguish between urgent and important tasks.

During my workshops, this is a very common phenomenon-

"All urgent tasks were once important, but because they were not attended to in a timely manner they have now become urgent."

Remember: "Address important tasks promptly to avoid them becoming urgent crises later."

Learn to Set Boundaries:

Establish clear boundaries between work and personal time. Communicate your availability to your team to manage expectations.

Let me share one real-time experience –

While working with a leading pharmaceutical company, I had the opportunity to closely collaborate with a highly intelligent and dedicated marketing manager. He showed great enthusiasm and commitment to the progress of his division and the brands he directly managed. I was thrilled to see his involvement and the growth of the brands. However, over time, I noticed that he began losing his enthusiasm and appeared less engaged. One day, I took him to a café to understand what was going on in his life and why he seemed less enthusiastic. I observed that he was bringing office work to his dining table, which led to stress and dissatisfaction both at work and in his personal life.

We discussed his future plans and his preferences. I suggested my friend the following-

Set clear work hours – 9.15 AM to 6 PM. Communicate this schedule to your team members now and suggest they finish the office-related work during this period.

Set up a dedicated workspace at home where you can conduct all your office-related work. When you leave this space, you shift your focus to personal activities.

Make sure to prioritize your personal time. Set aside time for activities you enjoy. For example, if you find joy in reading and cooking, consider planning a day to cook something special for your family.

He also made an agreement to communicate his boundaries to his family. He emphasized that he would let his wife know when he was leaving his office, and if he was at home, he would say that he was leaving his home office to join them for dinner. This way, he was able to allocate time for his family and reinforce the separation between his work and personal life.

My dear friend started practicing the same and after a couple of weeks, we again met at the same table in the café we met a few weeks ago.

I was happy to notice that stress levels were reduced dramatically, There was an improvement in productivity during work hours. He started enjoying time with his colleagues and his family.

This balanced approach helped him feel more fulfilled and less overwhelmed.

Leverage Technology:

Utilize apps and tools that help in scheduling, task management, and communication to save time. you can manage time well and can automate repetitive processes.

Self-Care and Well-Being:

Often, in your busy schedule, you miss to make time for exercise. People is sales don't get time for meals and mostly take junk food.

Make time for regular exercise, healthy eating, and proper sleep.

Engage in activities that recharge you.

Delegation:

Don't try to do everything on your own, learn the art of delegation. Trust your team with responsibilities, will allow you to focus on high-priority tasks and personal times.

Review:

Develop a mechanism to get feedback. You can seek feedback from family, friends, and colleagues to identify areas of improvement.

Regularly review your work-life balance and make adjustments as needed.

Remember: "By prioritizing tasks, setting boundaries, employing effective time management techniques, focusing on self-care, leveraging technology, and delegating responsibilities, you can create a harmonious balance that enhances both your professional and personal life. "

EFFECTIVE TIME MANAGEMENT

"Time is what we want most, but we use worst."

- William Penn

I often hear team members saying, "I don't have time, I am swamped, I couldn't manage it because I was overloaded." Do you encounter these situations? Everyone, in sales, knows that time management is crucial for success. Still, they are not able to manage time effectively. One thing is for sure salespeople have multiple responsibilities and I always respect their contribution. As a sales leader, I always used to help my team manage their time effectively. Time management is not about squeezing more tasks into your day; it is about ensuring your time is spent on the right tasks. This was my first piece of advice to them. I learned from my mentor who always encouraged us and used to say, "By mastering time management, you can achieve greater productivity and reduce stress." Once you learn time management then you will lead a more balanced and fulfilling professional life.

Key Techniques for Effective Time Management

1- Prioritization and Planning

As discussed earlier you can use the Eisenhower Matrix(Also known as the Urgent Important Matrix) to categorize tasks on urgency and importance.

Exercise:

List out all tasks and assign them to one of four categories:

Urgent and Important:

Important but not urgent:

Urgent but not important:

Neither urgent nor important

Design an action plan to address these tasks according to their priority and assign what your team can handle.

2- Set SMART Goals

Establish – Specific, Measurable, Achievable, Relevant, and Time-bound goals.

Break down larger goals into smaller, manageable tasks with clear deadlines.

Review your progress regularly and adjust your plan as needed to complete the task in time.

For example- you have a task to improve your sales by 20% in the next 90 days (quarter).

"This is specific, you can measure to ensure the numbers are increasing, Based on past performance and market conditions, and support a 20% increase in achievable and realistic, this goal aligns with the overall objective of company growth so it is relevant, you have to achieve this in next quarter so is time-bound."

How to break it down?

The first month- take a 5% increase in sales volume

The second month- take a 7% increase in sales volume

The third month -take an 8% increase in sales volume

You can have your weekly plans and those plans can be converted into daily tasks.

3- Delegation

First- identify tasks that can be delegated to others to free up your time for more critical activities.

Caution: Provide clear instructions and set expectations to ensure successful delegation.

Exercise-

You have a plan to celebrate the success of top performers and want to reward them at a function.

Set Objective –

Details- for example-

Date and Time-

Venue-

Invitations

Now delegate Responsibilities:

A- Who will handle venue booking and logistics-

What will be your instructions to him/her;

B- Who will handle Designing and the dispatch of invitations

What will be your instructions to him/her

C- Plan and event Agenda

Who will be responsible for this task?

What will be your instructions to him/her.

D- Set clear deadlines

Venue booked by--- Date/day

Invitation sent by -- Date/day

Event agenda finalized by--- Date/Day

Don't forget to plan a follow-up – schedule a check-in meeting /s to review progress and address any issues. Keep all concerned informed via email.

4- Use Technology

There are tools available for better time management. Employ Calendar tools to schedule, follow up meetings, and send reminders and updates.

Remember: "By clearly defining the tasks, responsibilities, and deadlines, you can effectively delegate tasks while ensuring accountability and progress towards the goal."

Key takeaways

- Prioritize tasks

- Allocate time

- Set SMART goals

- Delegate wisely

- Leverage Technology

As you master the art if managing your time effectively; it is equally important to recognize and address the impact of stress on your performance and well-being.

Remember- Time management and stress management go hand in hand, and by learning how to manage both, you can achieve a more balanced and productive life.

Sales professionals often experience high levels of stress due to demanding performance expectations, tight deadlines, and the pressure to meet or exceed sales targets. Some individuals struggle to effectively manage this stress, leading to burnout and decreased productivity.

By managing your time effectively, you can alleviate some of this stress and increase your productivity. Effective time management means-

Prioritization of tasks based on their importance and urgency

Setting realistic goals and

Allocating appropriate time for each activity.

This structured approach reduces the feeling of being overwhelmed and ensures that important tasks are completed on time. this will help you to maintain a healthier work-life balance, stay focused, and achieve better sales outcomes.

You can reduce your stress level by managing your time effectively.

I am suggesting a few practical tips to Manage Stress-

1- Prioritize and Plan – Start each day by identifying your top priorities and creating a to-do list. Schedule your tasks and allocate a specific time slot for each task. Be realistic while setting goals for the day.

2- Practice Mindfulness and Relaxation Techniques- Include mindfulness practices in your daily schedule, such as deep breathing exercises, meditation, or yoga to reduce stress and improve focus. Take short breaks throughout the day to practice these techniques. These techniques are very useful, especially during high-stress periods.

3- Maintain a Healthy Work-Life Balance –Set clear boundaries between work and personal life to ensure you have time to relax and recharge. Avoid taking office work to home or taking work-related calls during your personal time.

4- Prioritize Self-Care-Make self-care a non-negotiable part of your daily routine. Taking care of your physical and mental well-being is crucial for maintaining a balanced life.

Schedule regular activities that you enjoy and that help you relax, such as exercise, reading, or spending time with loved ones.

Eat well, sleep well, and take regular breaks during working hours.

Remember these important tips to effectively manage stress and increase productivity. Doing so can lead to improved performance and job satisfaction, and is crucial for maintaining a balanced work life. To truly excel and stay competitive in today's dynamic environment, commit yourself to continuous learning and professional development. Continuous learning empowers you to adapt, grow, and achieve long-term success.

Continuous Learning and Professional Development

"The only thing worse than training your employees and having them, leave is not training them and having them stay."

-Henry Ford

Selling is an ever-evolving process, and committing to continuous learning and professional development is not just an option but a necessity for those who want to excel in the profession.

In today's rapidly changing landscape, staying still is not an option, as a famous adage goes, "If you're not moving forward, you are going backward; there is no such thing as staying stagnant. Moving forward is not just a choice but a necessity to stay relevant and grow in this competitive world." To thrive and succeed, we must embrace change, seek new knowledge, and constantly push ourselves to improve.

Here are a few key points and actionable suggestions to help you on your journey of continuous improvement.

Key Points

1- **Adaptability-** The ability to adapt to new technologies, methodologies, and market demands is essential.

2- **Skill Enhancement-** Continuous learning helps in acquiring new skills and enhancing existing ones, making you more competent and versatile.

3- **Career Advancement-** A new role means new skills and more knowledge. Regularly updating your knowledge and skills can lead to promotions and career growth.

4- **Innovation-** Never means a discovery, but enabling you to bring fresh ideas and solutions to your organization. Lifelong learning fosters creativity and innovation.

5- **Personal Growth-** New learning always enhances your confidence and self-esteem. Keep learning for personal fulfillment.

6- **Competitive Edge-** Keeping up with industry trends and advancements helps you stay ahead of the competition.

Actionable Suggestions-

1- **Set Clear Learning Goals-** Identify areas where you need improvement or new skills you want to acquire to stay relevant. The Learning Goal must be SMART – Specific, Measurable, Achievable, Relevant, and Time-bound.

Example- You work in middle-level management and aspire to lead a team of senior leaders. You have identified public speaking as an area for improvement.

Exercise:

Make SMART Learning Goal-

Specific-

Measurable-

Achievable-

Relevant-

Time-bound-

Public speaking is crucial for professional development and effective communication, and by setting this SMART learning goal, you can create a clear, structured path to improve your public speaking skills.

2- **Create a learning Plan-** Develop a structured plan that outlines your learning objectives, resources, and timelines.

Exercise:

Your objective is to enhance skills in consultative selling to improve customer relationships and increase sales conversions by 10% within six months.

Step 1: Assess your current skill level

I suggest conducting a self-assessment and gathering feedback from your seniors and peers to identify strengths and areas of improvement in consultative selling.

Set timeframe: I will complete within..... week/days

Step 2: Set Specific Learning Goals

Goal 1- Basics---- Understand the principles and techniques of consultative selling.

Goal 2-

Goal 3-

Goal 4-

Step 3- Create a Learning Schedule

You can plan your weekly schedule

week 1

Week 2

Week 3

Week 4

Never forget to review progress against goals every week.

If need be adjust your plan.

Develop feedback mechanisms and regularly seek feedback from your seniors, peers, and customers.

Final assessment: evaluate improvement in sales conversions and customer feedback.

Apply Skills in Real-World Scenarios- Apply consultative selling techniques in all customer interactions and keep learning and stay updated with the latest trends and advancements in sales techniques and consultative selling.

I recommend you to read Book "**Spin Selling** " by Neil Rackham.

1- **Leverage Online resources-** Today, you have the liberty and opportunity to use online platforms like LinkedIn and YouTube at your convenience. You can find industry-related blogs, podcasts, and YouTube channels to stay updated.

2- **Attend Workshops and Seminars-** Participating in industry conferences, workshops, and seminars to gain hands-on experience and network with peers will make you more comfortable in using the acquired knowledge. Many organizations are providing professional development programs for their leaders, make yourself available for all such opportunities.

3- **Seek Mentorship-** As a progressive future ready sales leader in Industry find a mentor who can provide guidance, feedback, and support in your professional journey.

4- **Develop a habit of Reading–** Read books on subject, industry, and Journals related to your industry. Reading books is the best investment, returns are guaranteed once learning is applied.

5- **Apply What You Learn-** "Have you heard of seeing is believing?" – so implement new knowledge and skills in your daily work to reinforce learning, Take projects or tasks that challenge you and provide opportunities for practical application.

6- **Encourage Peer Learning-** You can establish a study group within your team, discussion forum, or learning sessions. Sharing knowledge and experience with colleagues fosters a collaborative learning environment.

With the help of the above tips, you not only enhance your own capabilities but also contribute to the growth and success of your organization. Be a lifelong learner and you will be well-equipped to navigate the challenges and opportunities of your career.

The exercises that you have done, will help you in systematically building your consultative selling skills.

With the application of new knowledge, you can achieve your sales goals and improve relationships.

Summary

'Sales Leadership Mastery' is a comprehensive guide designed to transform your personal and professional life by tapping into the potential within each of us. This book combines insightful stories, practical advice, and proven strategies to help you achieve success and fulfillment. We begin with Varun's story and then move to **Goal Setting,** where we emphasize the importance of clarity and specificity using the SMART framework. Through real-life examples, we illustrate how breaking down large goals into smaller, manageable tasks can lead to significant achievements.

Moving on to **Effective Sales Strategies,** we explore various techniques such as consultative selling, Value selling, and social selling. Using the story of Ramdas, a natural leader from his village, we demonstrate how these strategies can be applied in real-world scenarios to drive sales success.

In **Building High-Performing Teams,** we discuss the key elements of recruiting and training. Motivating and incentives. Ramdas' journey in organizing a village fair serves as an inspiring example of leadership and team management, highlighting the importance of collaboration and shared goals.

Nurturing Customer Relationships delves into the art of maintaining strong connections with customers. We share valuable insights and techniques to ensure customer loyalty and satisfaction, emphasizing the long-term benefits of these relationships.

Time Management and Stress Management are crucial for maintaining productivity and well-being. We provide practical tips and strategies to help you balance your work and personal life effectively, reducing stress and enhancing performance.

Finally, we focus on **Continuous Learning and Professional Development** stressing the importance of staying relevant and competitive in today's fast-paced world. Through SMART learning goals and clear learning plans, we guide you on how to keep advancing your skills and knowledge.

I am sure by reading and applying these techniques you will ensure your future is brighter than yesterday! Wishing you all the success on your journey to becoming an exceptional sales leader!

Thank you!!

About The Author

JP Pathak emerges as a seasoned professional in sales, management, training, and coaching, with a remarkable journey spanning over 35 years. As a dedicated student of sales and management, he has honed his expertise as a practitioner and mentor, guiding individuals to discover their "One Thing" that propels them toward realizing their dreams and purpose.

Throughout his extensive career, JP has navigated the intricacies of sales and marketing, earning a reputation as a sales superstar.

One of JP's distinctive qualities lies in his ability to simplify complex concepts, making them accessible and understandable for his audience. His training and coaching methods are infused with humor, creating an environment that fosters relaxation and comfort, even in challenging situations or when dealing with difficult-to-manage individuals.

JP's effectiveness as a trainer is not solely based on his vast experience but is enriched by his capacity to weave anecdotes and small stories into his teachings. These narratives serve as memorable lessons, ensuring that the knowledge imparted remains ingrained in the minds of his students for an extended period.

JP imparts wisdom and creates an engaging and enjoyable learning experience by incorporating humor and storytelling.

Beyond his professional endeavors, JP Pathak is a science graduate who shares his life with his wife and two daughters. His commitment extends beyond individual growth, as he actively contributes to developing people and organizations. Through his training and coaching initiatives, JP leaves an indelible mark on the journey of those he guides, fostering growth and success.

Other Books Written By The Author

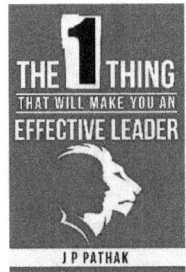

Click this book

Click this book

Click this book

Click this book

Click this book

Click this book

Disclaimer

This book is for informational purposes only. Readers acknowledge that the author does not render legal, financial, medical, or professional advice. The content within this book has been derived from various sources. Please consult a licensed professional before attempting any techniques outlined in this book.

By reading this document, the reader agrees that under no circumstances is the author responsible for any direct or indirect losses incurred due to the use of the information contained within this document, including but not limited to errors, omissions, or inaccuracies. Adherence to all applicable laws and regulations, including international, federal, state, and local governing professional licensing, business practices, advertising, and all other jurisdictions, is the sole responsibility of the purchaser or reader. Neither the author nor the publisher assumes any responsibility or liability on behalf of the purchaser or reader of these materials. Any perceived slight of any individual or organization is purely unintentional.

May I Ask You A Favor?

First, I want to say a big thanks for reading this book. You could have chosen any other book, but you took mine, and I appreciate this. I hope you have a few actionable insights that can positively impact your daily life.

Can I ask for 30 seconds more of your time?

I'd love it if you could leave a review of the book. That will help me grow my readership by encouraging folks to take a chance on my books.

Keeping it straight - reviews are the lifeblood of any author.

It will take less than a minute of your time but will tremendously help me reach out to more people. Kindly provide your review at the store you bought this book from. And I'd love to see your review. Thanks for your support.

www.ingramcontent.com/pod-product-compliance
Lightning Source LLC
Chambersburg PA
CBHW071833210526
45479CB00001B/111